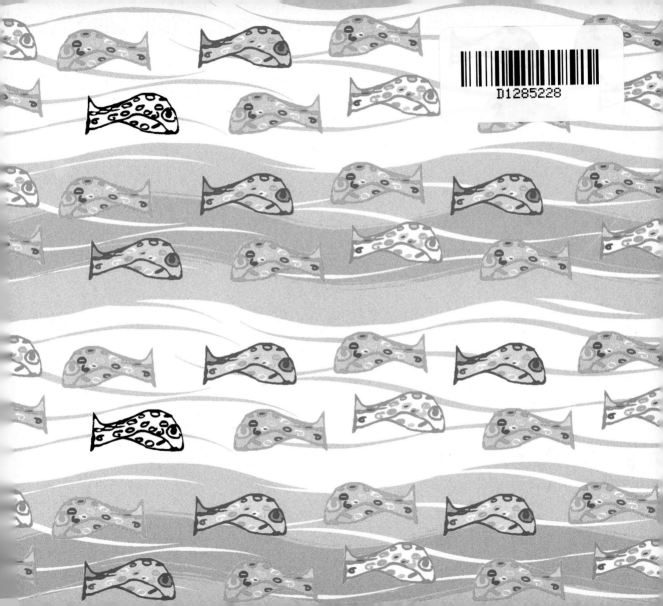

once upon an elephant

once upon an elephant

once upon an elephant

once upon an elephant

# JOHN LENNON
# real love
## THE DRAWINGS FOR SEAN

WITH AN INTRODUCTION BY YOKO ONO

ADAPTED BY AL NACLERIO FROM DRAWINGS BY JOHN LENNON

A LITTLE, BROWN BOOK

First published in the US by Random House, Inc. New York 1999
First published in Great Britain by Little, Brown and Company 1999

Copyright ©1999 by Yoko Ono Lennon.

ISBN 0 316 85164 7

A CIP catalogue record for this book is available from the British Library.

Printed and bound in Italy
by LEGO Spa

Little, Brown and Company (UK)
Brettenham House
Lancaster Place
London WC2E 7EN

In 1975, John became the father of a very special boy: Sean. John was ecstatic. "I'm going to raise this baby, Yoko. You do the business," he said. It was that simple.

John was a great daddy. He tried to do everything so right. I would come back from a hard day of work and find John waiting for me to report what took place that day.

"Sean was sneezing this morning. Maybe he's getting a cold."

"Sean needs more winter things. We have to go shopping."

Then pretty soon it became, "Sean did this all by himself." And John would proudly show me some squiggly lines Sean had drawn on paper. They were Sean's first drawings.

John had every one of Sean's drawings framed. We suddenly had many, many framed drawings by Sean adorning the walls of our Dakota apartment. Then I began to find John and Sean drawing together. John would draw something and explain to Sean what it was.

"This is a cat catnapping, Sean."

"Oh."

Then it was Sean's turn. He would show his drawings and explain, "This is a bus, and these are the people who want to get on the bus, but they can't because the bus is too small...so they're crying."

John would write what Sean had said underneath the drawings as titles. They became long, beautiful, and imaginative titles. Sometimes, John would ask Sean what he thought John was drawing. Sean would say, "That's a horsey," and that would become the title of John's drawing. They would make each other laugh, and that is how Sean learned the fun of drawing, the fun of doing things together with his dad, and the fun of life.

I hope you enjoy this book. It was done in the spirit of laughter...and lots and lots of love.

*Yoko Ono '99*

friends

a turtle winning by a hare

an elephant forgetting

crabs crabbing

fish winking

singing in harmony

a bird bath

a frog marching

a pigeon homing

a worm turning

a cat climbing

a horse peancing

the camol dances and having danced moves on

kangaroos crossing

sheep meadowing

a hippotato

a herd moving

a duck

a duck ducking

a small pig.
is a happy pig.

puppy love

an owl hooting

a horse laughing

a cat napping

an elephant counting

pecking order

collie flower

a walrus wading

seals singing

an egg hatching

a cat purring

the big dog frightens but not always

"Git along little dowgie."

a bird watching

a bird dreaming

a flock flying

a frog pondering

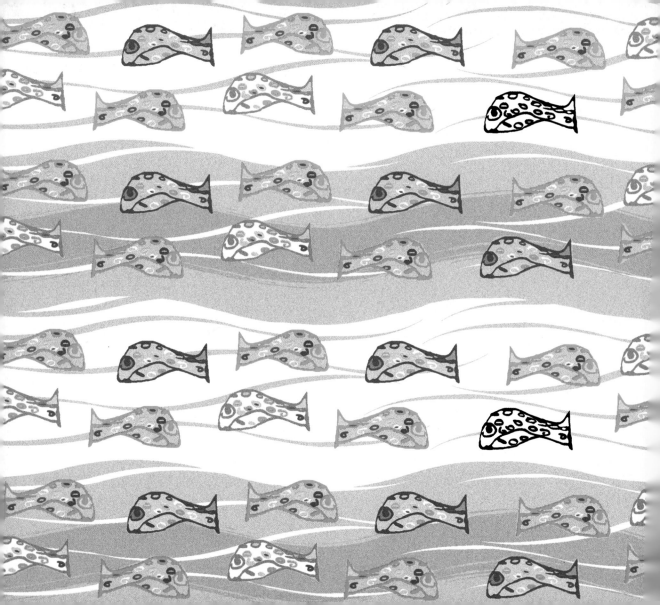